Fact Finders®

DISCOVER THE NIGHT SKY

EXPLORING
CONSTELLATIONS

BY SARA LATTA

Consultant:
Ilia Iankov Roussev, PhD

CAPSTONE PRESS
a capstone imprint

Fact Finders Books are published by Capstone Press,
1710 Roe Crest Drive, North Mankato, Minnesota 56003
www.mycapstone.com

Library of Congress Cataloging-in-Publication Data
Library of Congress Cataloging-in-Publication data is available on the Library of Congress website.

978-1-5157-8735-8 (library binding)
978-1-5157-8739-6 (paperback)
978-1-5157-8751-8 (eBook PDF)

Editorial Credits
Adrian Vigliano, editor; Veronica Scott, designer;
Wanda Winch, media researcher; Gene Bentdahl, production specialist

Photo Credits
Library of Congress: Prints and Photographs Division, 27 (inset); Science Source: David Nunuk, 26–27 (background); Shutterstock: Allexxandar, cover, angelinast, 15, Dainis Derics, 12, igordabari, 9, Ms Moloko, 13, Pavel Vakhrushev, starfield background, Phillip Rubino, 6–7, touyaoki, 28 (all), Triff, 29; Thinkstock: Stockphoto/baldas1950, 17, iStockphoto/Cylonphoto, 4–5 (background), iStockphoto/keitikei, 11, Photos.com, 5 (inset)

TABLE OF CONTENTS

CHAPTER 1

WHAT ARE CONSTELLATIONS?

Look up into the sky on a clear night, far from the lights of a city. You can see the moon, many stars, and maybe even a planet. Some of the stars look like bright diamonds. Others glow faintly. A few of them twinkle. You might look for groups of stars to form patterns. Join the stars in the patterns, like a dot-to-dot puzzle. Do you see a princess? Perhaps you see a dragon.

Thousands of years ago, stargazers around the world did the same. They saw clusters of stars that formed patterns. They thought they looked like animals or people. They told stories about the pictures they saw. These are the constellations.

The ancient Greek **astronomer** Ptolemy named 48 constellations. Today, there are 88 constellations. Together, all of the constellations fill the entire night sky. Each star we can see from Earth is part of some constellation.

astronomer—a scientist who studies stars, planets, and other objects in space

STARS AND GALAXIES

Stars are giant balls of hot gas. They make energy. We see that energy as light. Stars come in different sizes and colors. Our sun is a medium-sized yellow star. Stars that are larger than the sun are blue. They are very hot. Stars that are smaller than the sun are red. They are less hot.

Galaxies are made of stars. They are also made of clouds of gas and dust. We live in a galaxy called the Milky Way. If the sky is dark enough, you can see part of it. It looks like a cloudy white streak across the sky. The ancient Romans called it the Road of Milk.

LIGHT-YEARS APART

Some stars look close together in the night sky. In reality, they may be very far apart. One of the most familiar constellations is Orion. It is named after a hunter in Greek **mythology**. The three stars that form its belt are easy to find. The stars in Orion are hundreds of **light-years** away from each other. The two brightest stars in Orion are 400 light-years apart! Some look bright because they are closer to Earth. Others look bright because they are very large stars, but the naked eye can't see the difference.

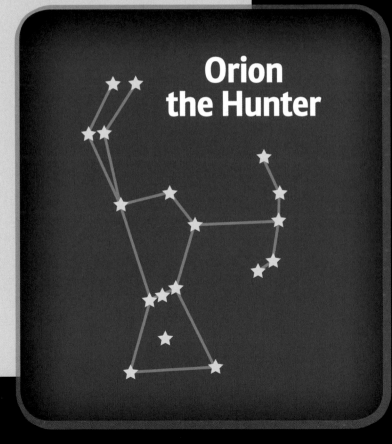

Orion the Hunter

mythology—old or ancient stories told again and again that help connect people with their past
light-year—a unit for measuring distance in space; a light-year is the distance that light travels in one year

CHAPTER 2

CONSTELLATIONS ON THE MOVE

Earth turns on its **axis** each day. This makes constellations appear to move across the sky from east to west each night. Earth makes a complete journey around the sun in one year. We see different constellations in each **hemisphere** with each season.

Some constellations appear close to Earth's poles. These are **circumpolar** constellations. People living in the Southern Hemisphere can see constellations near the South Pole all year. People living in the Northern Hemisphere can see constellations near the North Pole the year round. The lucky ones are the people living near the equator. They can see all of the constellations in the sky throughout the year! The constellations may appear high or low in the sky, depending on the season, but they are always there.

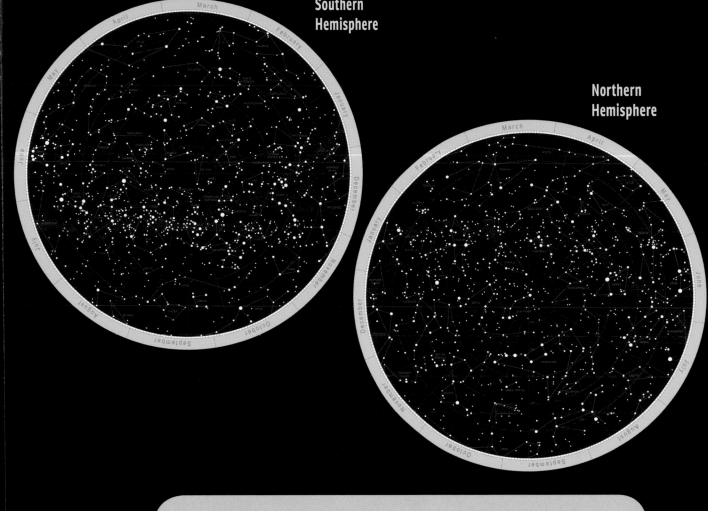

Southern Hemisphere

Northern Hemisphere

Most constellations are not near the poles. You can only see them during certain times of the year. They are seasonal constellations. You can see some of these constellations in both hemispheres.

axis—a real or imaginary line through the center of an object, around which the object turns

hemisphere—one half of the Earth; the equator divides the Earth into northern and southern hemispheres

circumpolar—the areas around one of Earth's poles

11

ANCIENT STARGAZERS

Around 5,000 years ago, Middle Eastern astronomers studied the stars and planets. They watched their positions and movements through the night sky as the seasons changed. They used this information to make calendars. These calendars helped farmers know when to plant their seeds. Travelers used the positions of the stars to guide them on their journeys.

These ancient astronomers had another reason for studying the night skies. They believed that the movements of the stars could help them understand the will of their gods. The planets, sun, and moon seemed to pass in front of a different constellation every month. Now we know that it is the other way around. As Earth **orbits** the sun, we look into space in different directions. That is why we see different constellations throughout the year.

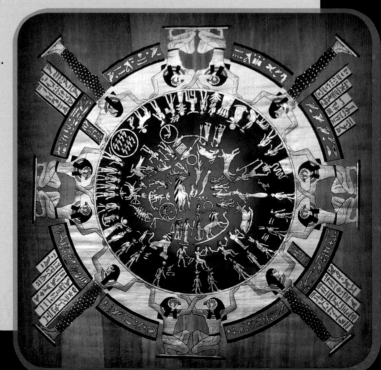

Egyptian calendar

These constellations became known as the Zodiac. The ancient astronomers thought that the constellations of the Zodiac affected events on Earth. This belief is the basis for **astrology**.

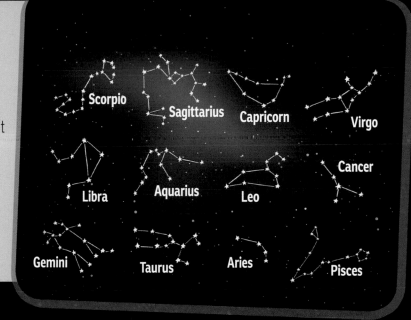

Scorpio
Sagittarius Capricorn
Virgo
Cancer
Libra Aquarius Leo
Gemini
Taurus Aries Pisces

Astronomy or Astrology?

Although astrology and astronomy have a shared history, they are very different. **Astronomy** is the scientific study of everything in outer space. Astrology is the belief that the movements of the stars and planets affect people and events on Earth. It is not a science.

Did You Know?

The word Zodiac means "circle of little animals."

orbit—the path an object follows as it goes around the sun or a planet

astrology—the study of the movements and positions of the planets and stars in the belief that they have an effect on events on Earth

astronomy—the study of stars, planets, and other objects in space

CIRCUMPOLAR CONSTELLATIONS IN THE NORTHERN SKY

There are many constellations visible in the Northern Hemisphere year round. Ursa Major, also called Great Bear, is one of them. It is one of the most famous constellations in the Northern Sky. Its seven brightest stars form a feature you may know: the Big Dipper. The Big Dipper is not a constellation. It is an **asterism**. The two stars on the outer edge of the dipper point directly to the North Star. Sailors used the North Star to find their way at sea. It was always in the north. It can help you figure out which way is north too!

Many cultures told stories about Ursa Major. The ancient Romans said that it was a beautiful woman named Callisto. They said a jealous goddess changed Callisto into a bear.

The tail of Ursa Minor, also called Little Bear, curves toward Ursa Major. The tail looks like a smaller version of the Big Dipper. People sometimes call it the Little Dipper. The North Star is at the very tip of its long tail. Roman legend says that Ursa Minor is Callisto's son. He was also turned into a bear.

Cassiopeia is shaped like a W (or an M, depending on the time of year). The constellation appears as a queen sitting on a chair, combing her hair.

Draco represents a dragon that was killed by the Greek warrior Hercules. Draco's body curls like a snake across the sky. It lies between Ursa Minor and Ursa Major.

CIRCUMPOLAR CONSTELLATIONS IN THE SOUTHERN SKY

Crux is the smallest of the 88 constellations. It points the way to the South Pole. It can help you figure out which way is south. The four brightest stars form the Southern Cross. They look like a kite.

Centaurus represents the centaur. In Greek mythology a centaur is half man, half horse. He holds a spear that he is using to kill a wolf. It contains the third brightest star in the sky, Alpha Centauri.

Carina represents part of a huge boat in the night sky. It contains the the night sky's second brightest star, Canopus.

Crux

CHAPTER 3

SEASONAL CONSTELLATIONS

There are many constellations that you can see only during certain times of the year. Here are just a few. Stargazers in the Northern Hemisphere may only be able to see the constellations at the top of each map. People in the Southern Hemisphere may only be able to see the constellations at the bottom of the maps.

CONSTELLATIONS FOR DECEMBER, JANUARY, AND FEBRUARY

Following close behind Orion, the Hunter, is one of his hunting dogs, Canis Major. The stars make the shape of a dog standing on its hind legs, chasing a rabbit. It is home to Sirius, also called the Dog Star. It is the brightest star in the sky.

Just under Orion's feet is Lepus, the Hare. He is always just out of Canis Major's reach.

Above Orion lies the large constellation, Taurus, the Bull. To the ancient Greeks, he represented the god Zeus. Zeus changed himself into a bull to get close to a lovely girl.

Above Orion on the other side is Gemini. The constellation is of twins Castor and Pollux, both from Greek myths. The twins, its two brightest stars, make it easy to find.

Gemini

Auriga

Canis Minor

Taurus

Orion

Monoceros

Canis Major

Lepus

Columba

Fornax

Puppis

Caelum

Pictor

Reticulum

Dorado

Horologium

CONSTELLATIONS FOR MARCH, APRIL, AND MAY

Boötes is also called the Herdsman. It follows Ursa Major around the North Pole. Some say that he is guiding a plow (the Big Dipper). Others say he is driving the Great Bear (Ursa Major) around the pole. Boötes' brightest star is Arcturus. The name means "bear keeper."

Virgo, or the Maiden, is the second largest constellation in the sky. It represents the Greek goddess of justice. She is also called the goddess of the harvest. In the Northern Hemisphere, she appears each spring during the planting and growing seasons.

Hydra, the Water Snake, is the largest constellation in the sky. Hydra was a monster killed by the Greek hero Hercules.

Cancer is the faintest of the 12 Zodiac constellations. It represents a crab sent by the goddess Hera to bite Hercules. One story says the angry Hercules kicked the crab all the way to the heavens.

Can you see what animal Leo represents? It looks like a great lion at rest. The gods placed it in the heavens because it was the King of the Beasts. Ancient people called its brightest star the "king star."

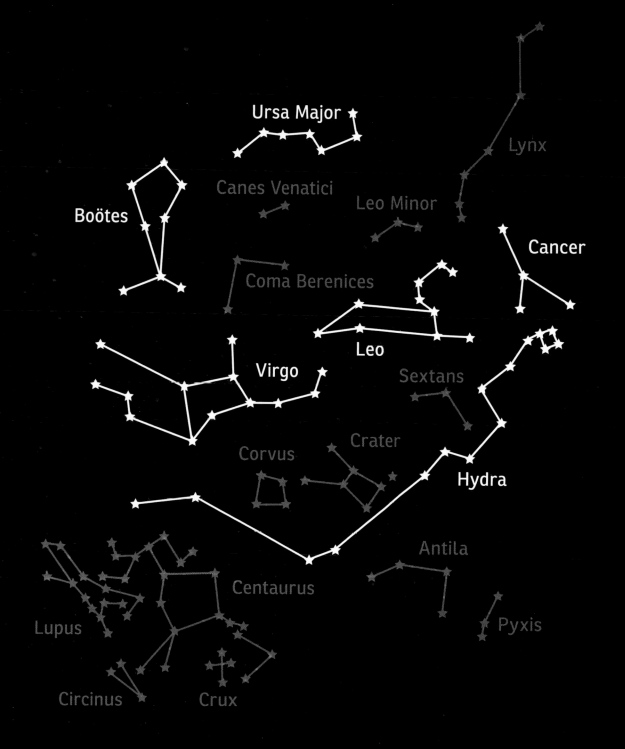

Ursa Major

Lynx

Boötes

Canes Venatici

Leo Minor

Cancer

Coma Berenices

Virgo

Leo

Sextans

Corvus

Crater

Hydra

Centaurus

Antila

Pyxis

Lupus

Circinus

Crux

CONSTELLATIONS FOR JUNE, JULY, AND AUGUST

Cygnus, the Swan, flies south through the Milky Way. It is easy to find. Four of its brightest stars form the Northern Cross.

In Greek mythology, Hercules is the son of the god Zeus. His father placed him in the heavens. There he kneels forever. A box of four stars forms his body.

Scorpius, the Scorpion, was ordered to kill Orion the Hunter. Its reward was a place in the starry sky. He lies opposite from Orion so that the two would never meet again. It is located near the center of the Milky Way. The bright star Antares marks its heart.

Sagittarius is another centaur. He holds a bow and arrow. In the constellation, he points his arrow straight at Scorpius. Inside Sagittarius is the asterism Teapot. Rising from the spout of Teapot is a cloud of "steam." That steam is the Milky Way.

Libra's name means "the weighing scales." It stands for the scales of justice held by the goddess in Virgo. It is the only constellation in the Zodiac that does not represent an animal or person.

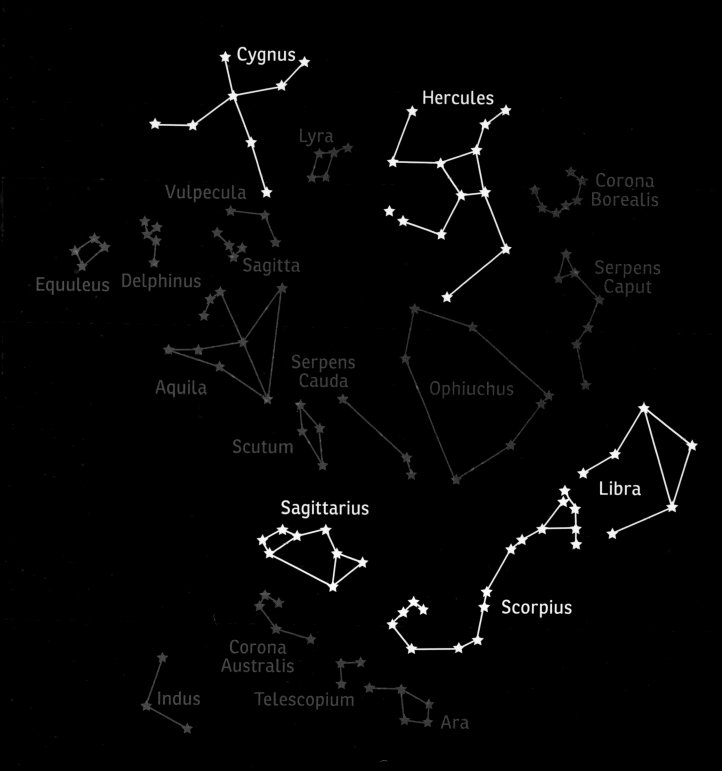

Cygnus

Hercules

Lyra

Corona
Borealis

Vulpecula

Serpens
Caput

Equuleus Delphinus

Sagitta

Aquila

Serpens
Cauda

Ophiuchus

Scutum

Libra

Sagittarius

Scorpius

Corona
Australis

Indus

Telescopium

Ara

CONSTELLATIONS FOR SEPTEMBER, OCTOBER, AND NOVEMBER

Andromeda was a beautiful princess. The hero Perseus rescued her from the sea monster Cetus. Her constellation lies just below and between her husband, Perseus, and her mother, Cassiopeia.

In Greek mythology Perseus killed the Medusa. The Medusa was a horrible monster with snakes for hair. The constellation Perseus is known for its yearly meteor shower.

The great winged horse, Pegasus, flies upside down in the northern night sky. He sprang from the neck of the Medusa when Perseus killed her. Pegasus' body is formed by a square of stars. The rest of the constellation shows only the horse's front legs, neck, and head.

Just east of Pegasus in the northern sky is Aries, the Ram. In Greek mythology Aries was a golden flying sheep. The curved line of the constellation represents his horns.

Aquarius is the water-carrier. He lies between Pegasus and Capricornus. In Greek mythology he was a boy who poured drinks for the gods.

Greek myths say that Capricornus, or the Goat, is half goat, half fish. This strange sea-goat constellation lies south of Aquarius.

Pisces represents a pair of fish. They are joined by a cord. This constellation lies just south of Pegasus.

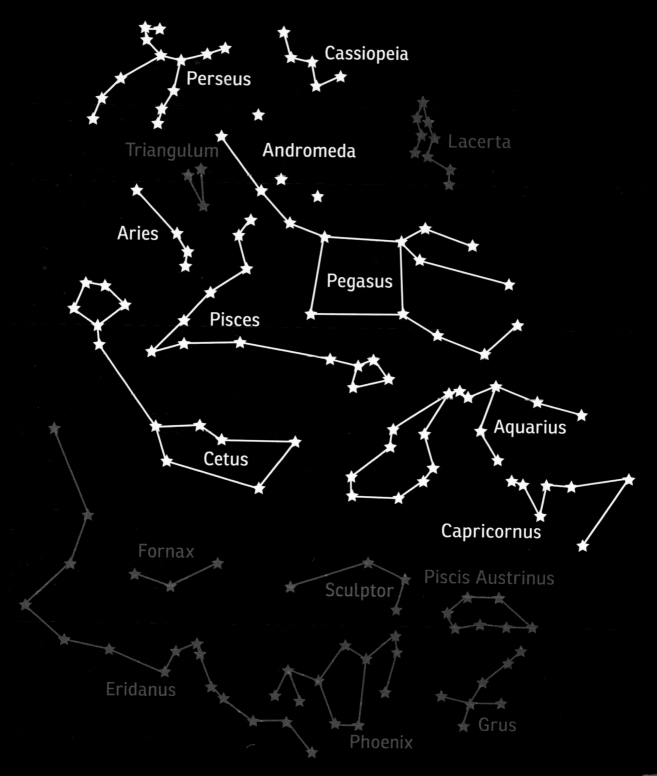

Cassiopeia

Perseus

Triangulum

Andromeda

Lacerta

Aries

Pegasus

Pisces

Cetus

Aquarius

Capricornus

Fornax

Piscis Austrinus

Sculptor

Eridanus

Phoenix

Grus

CHAPTER 4

CONSTELLATIONS IN OTHER CULTURES

Sky watchers from other cultures told stories about the stars too. The Southern Cross is an important constellation to many people. One tribe from Australia saw the Southern Cross as the head of a great emu. The emu is a large, flightless bird from Australia. In Peru the ancient Incans called the constellation the Stair. Natives of New Zealand called it the Anchor.

The early Hawaiians were skilled sailors. They used the movements of the stars to steer their boats thousands of miles in the open ocean. One of their star stories was about the hero Maui. Maui made a magical fish hook to haul the Hawaiian Islands up out of the ocean.

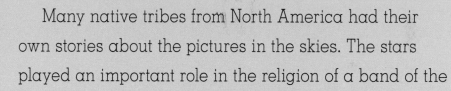

Many native tribes from North America had their own stories about the pictures in the skies. The stars played an important role in the religion of a band of the Pawnee Indians. They called a ring of stars in the sky "The Council of Chiefs."

The ancient Chinese, too, looked to the sky for signs from their gods. They had their own zodiac. It was divided into four sections. Each section was linked to the seasons. The Blue Dragon of the East was spring. The Red Bird of the South was summer. The White Tiger of the West was autumn. The Black Turtle of the North was winter.

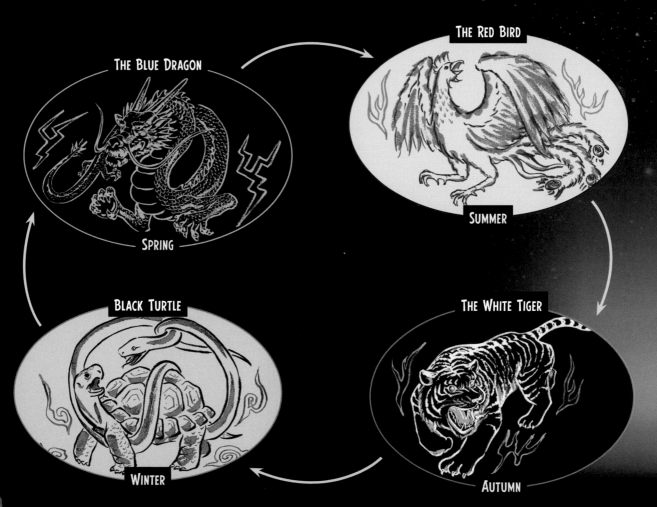

THE BLUE DRAGON

SPRING

THE RED BIRD

SUMMER

BLACK TURTLE

WINTER

THE WHITE TIGER

AUTUMN

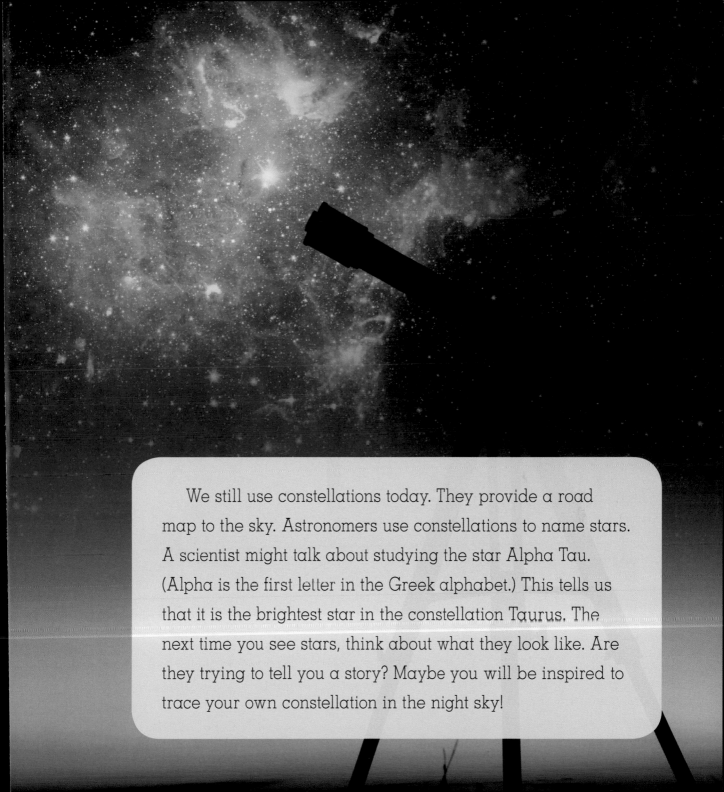

We still use constellations today. They provide a road map to the sky. Astronomers use constellations to name stars. A scientist might talk about studying the star Alpha Tau. (Alpha is the first letter in the Greek alphabet.) This tells us that it is the brightest star in the constellation Taurus. The next time you see stars, think about what they look like. Are they trying to tell you a story? Maybe you will be inspired to trace your own constellation in the night sky!

GLOSSARY

asterism (AS-tur-ism)—a small group of stars within a larger constellation

astrology (uh-STRAH-Luh-jee)—the study of the movements and positions of the planets and stars in the belief that they have an effect on events on Earth

astronomer (uh-STRAH-nuh-muhr)—a scientist who studies stars, planets, and other objects in space

astronomy (AS-tur-ism)—the study of stars, planets, and other objects in space

axis (AK-siss)—a real or imaginary line through the center of an object, around which the object turns

circumpolar (suhr-kuhm-POH-lur)—the areas around one of Earth's poles

hemisphere (HEM-uhss-fihr)—one half of the Earth; the equator divides the Earth into northern and southern hemispheres

light-year (LITE-yihr)—a unit for measuring distance in space; a light-year is the distance that light travels in one year

mythology (mi-THOL-uh-jee)—old or ancient stories told again and again that help connect people with their past

orbit (OR-bit)—the path an object follows as it goes around the sun or a planet

READ MORE

Hunter, Nick, *Stars and Constellations. The Night Sky: and Other Amazing Sights.*
Chicago: Heinemann Library, 2014.

Rey, H.A., *Find the Constellations.* Boston: HMH Books for Young Readers, 2016.

Zschock, Martha, *Constellations Scratch & Sketch: An Art Activity Book.*
White Plains, N.Y.: Peter Pauper Press, 2014.

INTERNET SITES

Use FactHound to find Internet sites related to this book.

Visit *www.facthound.com*

Just type in 9781515787358 and go.

CRITICAL THINKING QUESTIONS

1. Why can a starwatcher in Montana (North America) see the constellation Leo in April but not in October?

2. Why is it difficult to find constellations near the lights of a big city?

3. How can travelers use constellations to navigate without a compass or other guidance systems?

INDEX